Ocean Power

THE UNIVERSITY OF ARIZONA PRESS

© 1995 Ofelia Zepeda

www.uapress.arizona.edu

Library of Congress Cataloging-in-Publication Data
Zepeda, Ofelia.
Ocean power : poems from the desert / Ofelia Zepeda.
p. cm. — (Sun Tracks : v. 32)
ISBN 978-0-8165-1541-7 (pbk. : alk. paper)
1. Indians of North America—Arizona. 2. Tohono O'odham
Indians. 3. Deserts—Arizona. I. Title. II. Series.
PS501.S85   vol. 32
[PS3576.E64]
810.8'0054 s—dc20
[811'.54]   94-18732

Publication of this book is made possible in part by a grant from
the Arizona Commission on the Arts through appropriations
from the Arizona State Legislature and grants from the National
Endowment for the Arts.

Manufactured in the United States of America on acid-free,
archival-quality paper containing a minimum of 30% post-
consumer waste and processed chlorine free.

16   15   14   13   12   8   7   6   5

OCEAN POWER
Poems from the Desert

Ofelia Zepeda

The University of Arizona Press / Tucson

Volume 32

Sun Tracks

An American Indian Literary Series

SERIES EDITOR

Ofelia Zepeda

EDITORIAL COMMITTEE

Vine Deloria, Jr.

Larry Evers

Joy Harjo

N. Scott Momaday

Emory Sekaquaptewa

Leslie Marmon Silko

Contents

Introduction

Things That Help Me Begin to Remember

In the dark shadows of an early summer morning, the muffled movements in the outdoor kitchen filter around the corner where we sleep. My mother and her mother begin preparations for the day. The kerosene lamp is the only light until the fire is started in the adobe cooking stove. The crackling of dry desert wood always sounds the same, its odor is always familiar. The wood lights quickly and heats up fast. The pots and pans hanging on the saguaro rib fence make soft clinks in the darkness. With muffled movements the two women prepare fresh tortillas, eggs, beans, and coffee for breakfast. They also prepare food for my uncle to take for his noonday meal. With the same quiet movements, the women set pots of food on to boil for the family's noon meal.

▪▪

Like the people before them, these women gauged the movement of the summer sun and the amount of work that needed to be done. They worked carefully to get their heaviest household work done, work that would be too much

I

to carry out under the late mid-morning or afternoon sun. The women planned their day around the heat and the coolness of the summer day. They knew the climate and felt confident in it. They knew the weather and its movements.

They talked about it in their own way. They often laughed out loud at the dry thunderstorms that threatened, but were too weak to do any good. And they laughed in childlike manner when a thunderstorm arrived with all its bounty. During these storms they sat quietly watching the rivulets form on the dirt walls and small waterfalls pour from the edges of ramadas. I remember how these adults laughed at anyone who got caught in the rain and came running in drenched. They laughed at the way he or she might look, but they also seemed to laugh at the delight of the wetness, the thorough wetness. They laughed at the mud, the way it formed so instantly, magically, from just a few drops of rain. They laughed at the way it coagulated between the children's toes.

Like so many others, these women talked about the movements of potential rain clouds. They watched the sky more in the summer. They spoke of the clouds, the ones *"mat aṣ e-paḍc"* (that just ruined themselves). These were the clouds that fell apart, that did not build up enough to cause rain. These were clouds that people said *"aṣ t-iatogĭ"* (just lied to us).

❚❚

Even before the clouds become visible, the other sensory nerves are affected. The odor of wet dirt precedes the rain. It is an aroma so strong for some that it wakes them from sleep. People like to breathe deeply of this wet dirt smell. It is the smell not only of dirt but of the dry bark of mesquite and other acacias. It is the smell of the fine dust that must settle on all the needles and spines of saguaro and all manner of cactus, the dust that settles on the fine leaves of ocotillo and other leafed plants. It is all those things that give off an aroma only when mixed by rain. It is all breathed in deeply.

I I

I remember seeing the women do this. And when they breathed in, they would remark about the *si s-wa'us u:wï* (it smells like wetness). To the women, my mother, my grandmother, there was beauty in all these events, the events of a summer rain, the things that preceded the rain and the events afterward. They laughed with joy at all of it.

Simultaneously, they had an ever-abiding fear and respect for the other components of rain—lightning and flood. With the lightning, women stood and pressed themselves against the adobe walls, becoming part of the buildings. They shut their eyes to the brilliant, electrically charged colors of white and blue. They screamed at the thunder that followed. The men sat quietly, waiting it all out, powerless, all of them tasting the magnetized air at the back of their throats.

Flooding waters were a cautious gift. The women's fields were saturated with run-off from washes that flooded; but then there were the unusual cloudbursts or the continual rains that caused only flooding and damage. I have memories of flooding when my father worked the cotton fields. The cotton fields held hidden dangers. During sudden cloudbursts and extended rainfall, the volume of water in irrigation ditches multiplied in minutes. The workers in the fields ran to get across the ditches before the water rose too high or currents ran too swiftly. Perhaps they looked like pack animals crossing rushing rivers. The men rushed, each one helping the other to get across. Some of them fell into the water, grasping at the opposite bank for safety. The ditches held only five feet of water, but the current moved too quickly for anyone to be safe. The wives of the men waiting at home surely must have felt relief when my father's pickup truck came up the road with the men in the back. This broke the tension.

3

∎ ∎

The rain breaks the tension for the desert. Relief. Cycles continue.

∎ ∎

These are only some of the events that help me begin to remember, and the poems I include here are of some of those memories. Some of the poems and memories run into each other. Like my parents, I am aware of the movements of weather — rain in particular. I don't know why. It is just that way. So, many of the pieces in this collection are about events around rain — rain in the desert and events that result.

Others are stories about people, my extended family and relatives. I must apologize to my sisters if I make them cry by helping them to remember. I don't mean to make them cry. I only intend to help capture some of our collective memory.

As for the pieces that are written in O'odham, for the moment I will simply say that O'odham is my first language. I feel confident in the language and so am able to create pieces solely in my first language. Some of the pieces here have versions that also appear in English; however, all of the O'odham pieces originated in O'odham. For the pieces that appear only in O'odham, the English versions never occurred, so no versions of them exist in that language. The O'odham pieces could be meant for the small but growing number of O'odham speakers who are becoming literate. Here, then, is little bit of O'odham literature for them to read.

Finally, I acknowledge all those who continue to help me begin to remember. My family here in Tucson, Tony and Christina. My family and relatives who still live and work in the cotton fields of Stanfield, Arizona.

And I acknowledge my relatives and family who have already gone, those who lived farther south of here. Those who participated in the ritual of pulling down the clouds and fixing the earth.

All those who knew how to live toward the direction of the ocean.

'I-huḍiñ g Cewagĭ

Pulling Down the Clouds

Pulling Down the Clouds

Ñ-ku'ibaḍkaj 'ant 'an ols g cewagĭ.
With my harvesting stick I will hook the clouds.
'Ant o 'i-wañ'io k o 'i-huḍiñ g cewagĭ.
With my harvesting stick I will pull down the clouds.
Ñ-ku'ibaḍkaj 'ant o 'i-siho g cewagĭ.
With my harvesting stick I will stir the clouds.

With dreams of distant noise disturbing his sleep,
the smell of dirt, wet, for the first time in what seems like months.
The change in the molecules is sudden,
they enter the nasal cavity.

He contemplates that smell.
What is that smell?
It is rain.

Rain somewhere out in the desert.
Comforted in this knowledge he turns over
and continues his sleep,
dreams of women with harvesting sticks
raised toward the sky.

O'odham Dances

'E-atkĭ 'ep 'ai mat o 'e-keihi g o'odham
o 'e-keihi kut hab masma ab o 'i ha-miabĭ g ju:kĭ
'apt ge cuhug oidk o ka:d mat hab o kaijjid:

"'oig 'o, 'oig 'o
'at hahawa o ma:si
'oig 'o, 'oig 'o
'am o aṣkia wi'is g ñeñe'i
'oig 'o, 'oig 'o
'at hahawa o 'i-ceṣ g taṣ
'oig 'o, 'oig 'o
'am o aṣkia wi'is g s-cuhug
'oig 'o, 'oig 'o."

It is the time for the ritual.
To dance, to sing so that rain may come,
so that the earth may be fixed one more time.
Throughout the night,
a night too short for such important work,
the people converge energies.
They call upon the night.
They call upon the stars in the darkness.
They call upon the hot breezes.
They call upon the heat coming off the earth.
They implore all animals.
The ones that fly in the sky.
The ones that crawl upon the earth.
The ones that walk.
The ones that swim in the water and
the ones that move in between water, sky, and earth.
They implore them to focus on the moisture.
All are dependent.
From the dark dryness of the desert,
on that one night the call of the people is heard.
It is heard by the oceans, winds, and clouds.
All respond sympathetically.
Throughout the night you hear the one who is assigned yelling:

>   "'oig 'o, 'oig 'o
>   before it becomes light
>   'oig 'o, 'oig 'o
>   there are still songs to be sung

'oig 'o, 'oig 'o
before the sun comes up
'oig 'o, 'oig 'o
there is still a little bit of night left.

With the dawn we face the sunrise.
We face it with all our humility.
We are mere beings.
All we can do is extend our hands toward the first light.
In our hands we capture the first light.
We take it and cleanse ourselves.
We touch our eyes with it.
We touch our faces with it.
We touch our hair with it.
We touch our limbs.
We rub our hands together, we want to keep this light with us.
We are complete with this light.
This is the way we begin and end things.

Ju:ǩĭ Ñeʼi

Wa nt o m-ñeʼi g ju:ǩĭ ñeʼi.
Wa nt o ñ-keihi m-we:hejeḍ.

I would sing for you rain songs.
I would dance for you rain dances.

Na:nko Ma:s Cewagi

Cloud Song

Ce:daghim ʼo ʼab wu:ṣañhim.
To:tahim ʼo ʼab wu:ṣañhim.
Cuckuhim ʼo ʼab him.
Wepeghim ʼo ʼabai him.

Greenly they emerge.
In colors of blue they emerge.
Whitely they emerge.
In colors of black they are coming.
Reddening, they are right here.

Wind

The wind was whipping my clothes harshly around me,
slapping me,
hurting me with the roughness.
The wind was strong that evening.
It succeeded in blowing my clothes all around me.
Unlike others I revel in it.
I open my mouth and breathe it in.
It is new air,
air, coming from faraway places.
From skies untouched,
from clouds not yet formed.
I breathe in big gasps of this wind.
I think I know a secret, this is only the opening act
of what is yet to come.

I see it coming from a long distance away.
A brown wall of dust and dirt,
moving debris that is only moments old,
debris that is hundreds of years old.
All picked up in a chaotic dance.
The dust settles in my nostrils.
It clings to the moisture in my mouth.
It settles on my skin and fine hairs.

Memories of father and how he sat in front of the house
watching the wind come.
First he would smell it, then he would see it.
He would say, "Here he comes,"
much in the same way as if he saw a person on the horizon.
He would sit.
Letting the wind do with him what it will,
hitting him with pieces of sand.
Creating a fine layer all over him.
Finally when he could not stand it any longer
he would run into the house, his eyes shut,
shut against the tears getting ready to cleanse his eyes.
We all laughed at his strange appearance.
He also reveled in this wind.
This was as close as he could get to it,
to join it, to know it, to know what the wind brings.
My father would say, "Just watch, when the wind stops,
the rain will fall."

The story goes.

Wind got in trouble with the villagers.

His punishment was that he should leave the village forever.

When he received his sentence of exile

Wind went home and packed his things.

He packed his blue winds.

He packed his red winds.

He packed his black winds.

He packed his white winds.

He packed the dry winds.

He packed the wet winds.

And in doing this he took by the hand

his friend who happened to be blind,

Rain.

Together they left.

Very shortly after, the villagers found their crops began to die.

The animals disappeared,

and they were suffering from hunger and thirst.

To their horror the people realized they were wrong

in sending Wind away.

And like all epic mistakes it took epic events

to try to bring Wind back.

In the end it was a tiny tuft of down

that gave the signal that Wind was coming back.

With him was his friend, Rain.

He brought back the dry wind,

the cold wind,
the wet wind,
the cool wind,
but in his haste,
he forgot
the blue wind,
the white wind,
the red wind,
and the black wind.

Black Clouds

Black clouds lay off in the distance.
Like black buzzards, flying, far away.
Making noise, rumbling.
Black clouds
drifting off in the distance.
Like black buzzards, flying, so far away.
Rumbling, thundering.
Suddenly they descend.

The Floods of 1993 and Others

Old trees uprooted,
grasses, twigs, and branches,
all forced,
all pointing with limbs in the same direction,
as if telling us,
the one that did this to us went that way.

Barrel cactus,
hanging in uncactuslike manner,
upside down in between tree trunks and large branches.

They silently scream,
"My roots are still good, put me in the rocky soil."
The screams are inaudible.
Even if every curved thorn joins in

the Park Service employees don't hear them.

Or if they do, they ignore them.

Too busy repairing concrete.

Bear grass.

With meticulously groomed hair.

Hair, just so.

Every strand in place.

The flooding water though has done its damage.

The groomed hair is now tangled, matted,

indistinguishable shapes.

Those sitting in a row, having the appearance of Diana Ross and the Supremes
    of the '60s.

Stiff, bouffant hair,

all pointing in the same direction.

Redundantly saying, "The one that did this to us went that way."

Some gathered along the rocky borders,

posing possible solutions.

How to fix the hair.

Another flood perhaps, going in the opposite direction.

Highly unlikely.

Some secretly wished for the ultimate disaster. Fire.

One which they would survive with renewed opportunity.

They concurred.

Life is not so bad to have hair like a bird's nest.

Gone are the days of arrogant, strutting comparisons.

Pigs.

"Pigs," my friend remarked,

"I hated taking care of those pigs anyway.

"I was never so happy as when I saw them floating down the river when it
  flooded.

In fact, I think I even waved. I was just a kid then."

Remains.

His ashes are now at the bottom of the hill.

The rain has washed them down,

mixing them back into the dirt from where he came.

He screamed those silent screams.

You thought you heard them in between his laughter.

It was a confused message. Like many messages from adolescents.

A fifteen-year-old can't be expected to understand them all.

The ashes have found their way to the four directions by now.

Mixed with clouds that bring rain.

Or perhaps they have made their way to the Gila River when it flows in Pima
  country.

Surely some have made their way to the big rivers, floating on down to Mexico,

becoming part of the sandy, warm beach where you smile at the crabs that run
  sideways.

Trails.

It is all mere dirt and rock.

Wiped off the side of a mountain as if by a child playing in a sandbox.

Tony and Ken run softly.

Their lungs rhythmically, quietly screaming.

Following the canyon trail loop.

A trail familiar with every turn, every incline.

They welcome every gentle pain the rocks hand them.

And like two sighted men suddenly gone blind,

they feverishly try to find their trail.

Down on hands they grope for rocks that should have been there.

They feel trees that weren't there before.

The trail has fallen off the side of the mountain.

They balk in their rhythm and look at the side of a mountain,

a side that wasn't there before.

An inconvenience at best.

They debate which way to go that would be closest to the original trail

Their time cannot be slowed by this act of nature.

Grasses.

Grasses caught in tufts of all sizes,

hanging from every limb that was in the water's path.

All debris carried by water, reshaping a canyon.

Limb caught upon limb in wild, frozen dance postures.

Sand piled in places and manner unaccustomed.

Nature's features reshaped, molested by a watery monster.

Touching everything except the U.S. Park Service picnic tables.

Heavy concrete remains steadfast in the midst of nature's war zone.

Boulders.

Boulders, the size of small cars.

Now sit in the midst of empty streambeds,

quizzically contemplating how to accessorize.

The Department of Transportation and Flood Control.

201 North Stone Avenue, Tucson, Arizona.

Emergencies after 5 P.M. call.

Inquiries.

Flooding.

Road Maintenance.

Administration.

Community Relations.

Flood Control and Planning Development.

Operations Maintenance Division.

Emergencies after 5 P.M. call.

Emergencies after 5 P.M. call.

Permits.

Flood plain.

Grading.

Highway use.

Hillside.

Property management.

Emergencies after 5 P.M. call.

Emergencies after 5 P.M. call.

Please leave a message after the scream.

Cewagĭ

Pi ṣa:muñim 'ab dahă.
'ab dahă kc 'ab beihim g gewkdag
'ab beihim 'amjeḍ g s-ke:g hewel.
'I:da gewkdag mo na:nko ma:s.
'I:da gewkdag mo ḍ 'ep ge'e tatañ.
'I:da tatañ mat 'ab amjeḍ o si 'i-hoi g jeweḍ.
'I:da tatañ mo we:s 'an 'i t-bijimidahim.

Summer clouds sit silently.
They sit, quietly gathering strength.
Gathering strength from the good winds.
This strength that becomes the thunder.
The thunder so loud it vibrates the earth.
The thunder that surrounds us.

Irrigation Ditches

The Man Who Drowned in the Irrigation Ditch

She always got mad at him

every time he came home in the middle of the morning

with his pant legs wet.

She knew he had fallen in the ditch again.

His legs were not strong enough to be straddling ditches.

He was too old to be walking over temporary dikes.

She wished he didn't do that, but sometimes he had to.

She sometimes imagined him falling over backward in one of the irrigation

    ditches,

his head hitting hard cement,

his body slowly sinking into the water.

Water that was only three feet deep.

A harmless three feet of water,

where children played,

and ladies sometimes sat and dipped their feet,
especially on hot summer evenings.
She knew he would drown,
she knew it was bound to happen sometime.

As far as the eye could see,
flat, green fields appearing to end at the foot of distant mountains.
Mountains, a reminder of what the fields once looked like.
Fields saturated with water pulled from its secret storage place
beneath the earth's surface.

We are called "the people of the cotton fields"
because of the labor our families did.
For us there was no reservation, no Housing & Urban Development, no tribal
    support.
We were a people segregated in row houses
all lined up along the roads of our labor.

It is a muggy summer evening.
My father, my sister, and I sit on the east side of the house finding shade
    against the still-hot setting sun.
The change from brilliant white sun to blue and gold sunset and finally,
to warm darkness, a change we anticipate for brief relief.

On this evening the anticipation is shattered.
A boy comes to the house. He gestures for my father to come to him, out of
    our hearing.
With what the boy says to him my father moves quickly.
As quickly as his stiff back and legs can move him.

Back and legs broken and fused from when he was a cowboy.

He rushes by, throwing the kitchen door open, grabbing his hat.

He gets into his truck and drives away.

We pay him no mind other than for the fact that he is rushing.

A second later my mother comes out of the house and with a single motion
pulls her apron off.

In a tone I recognize as signifying something is wrong, she instructs us to
come with her.

She starts in the direction of a cotton field a few hundred yards from our house.

My sister and I walk beside her.

Saying nothing.

Her hands wring the towel she carries with her.

This towel, a multipurpose kind of thing.

Women carry it to fan themselves,

to wipe sweat, to cover their heads and eyes from sunlight, to shoo away kids,
dogs, flies.

I remember once a student of mine, out of habit, brought her towel with her
to summer school at the university.

Whenever we see each other on campus during a summer session we always
laugh about it.

We continue to walk, stepping over the ends of rows of cotton.

Rows of cotton my family and I know well.

In early summer we walk the rows to thin out the growth,

and later we walk to chop the weeds somehow immune to chemicals.

And in the winter, at least before the machinery, we pick the cotton from their
stalks.

Now I can't begin to imagine how many miles we have all walked,
up and back, up and back along these rows.

We walk alongside her.
The setting sun maintains a continuous pounding on our backs,
the humidity from the damp fields is warm, it rests on our shoulders like tired,
   sweaty arms.
She heads toward the irrigation ditch.
The ditch is dirt, not cement, it is wide, muddy, and slippery.
The water is shallow.
I see my father's truck pulling up on the opposite side.
In the front seat there are women, and in the back, men.
The men wedge their feet in between plastic and aluminum irrigation pipes,
   mud-caked shovels, boots, and hoes.
Equipment in the back of his truck all for the purposes of working fields.
I remember the hoe he carried.
It was big, with a blade that held an edge well and got the work done.
I recall purchasing a hoe for my home and being particularly unsatisfied with
   the craftsmanship.
"They call this a hoe?" I said to my husband. It had a skinny neck, and no
   blade to speak of.
The handle was too thin, causing blisters.
Once in awhile I look around for the type of hoe my father carried. I found one
   once, but didn't have money to buy it.

In slow motion,
weighed down by the heat,
the women begin to slide across the bench of the pickup truck.

32

They slowly step out of the cab, appearing as a single long strand of woman,
    emerging.
In cautious unison they walk toward the edge of the ditch.
My mother, as if connected to them by an invisible string,
is pulled toward them from the opposite side.
Their movement is dreamlike. They peer into the muddy water.
And as if with a shared nervous system, their hands motion the towel each is
    carrying,
motion it to just above their eyes, covering their faces.
With a single vocal act they release from their depths a hard, deep, mournful
    wail.
This sound breaks the wave of bright summer light above the green cotton
    fields.

Her Hair Is Her Dress

She lived to be over one hundred years old.
She told her children, "When I die, make a pillow for me out of my hair."
She had saved her hair all those years.
She used to say, "I don't want to be scratching through the ashes looking for
    my hair."
In the end her head did rest on her pillow of hair.

She pulls and twists, braiding.
Talking, pulling words down the length of the hair.
Make the part straight, be sure she is in balance.
Follow the path to the rabbit's nest.
That place at the base of the skull.
That private place that is hers alone.
That other place where the heartbeat is visible through the skin.

A tender place. Vulnerable.

Hit her there, her knees buckle and she falls face down at your feet.

A place so tender only a baby rabbit might sleep.

Hair Stolen

It happened at the rodeo parade.

Someone cut her hair. Someone, a crazy person, a witch maybe.

Took her hair for a sacrifice, for decoration, for a magic charm perhaps.

Since then there were other stories.

One woman said someone took her hair in a movie theater.

She said, "It was my fault because I like to throw it over the back of the chair."

Another said, "I was riding the Greyhound bus home. I fell asleep and was
    dreaming of home.

I dreamt of how my sister used to comb my long hair for me. She used to pull
    it hard.

When I woke I found over twelve inches gone."

These women will search the ashes for their hair when they leave this earth.

Don't Be Like the Enemy

This is what she said, "Don't be like the enemy, keep your hair out of your
    face."
Tie it back, don't be like a savage.
Let them see your face, let them know the light in your eyes.
But don't stare.
Cover your face by lowering it slightly.
Just don't use your hair, don't be like the enemy.

Long Hair

On the other side they sing and dance in celebration.

When we get there our hair must be long so that they recognize us.

Our hair is our dress.

It is our adornment.

We make sure it is long so they recognize us.

Hairpins

They glitter like broken glass on black asphalt.
Dime store hairpins of clear plastic, rhinestones, glass diamonds, and multi-
 colored aluminum strips.
Little hairpins, plastic combs all placed at intervals around her hair.
They glisten, sparkle, throwing light all around her,
giving her a halo.

Bury Me with a Band

My mother used to say, "Bury me with a band,"
and I'd say, "I don't think the grave will be big enough."
Instead, we buried her with creosote bushes,
and a few worldly belongings.
The creosote is for brushing her footprints away as she leaves.
It is for keeping the earth away from her sacred remains.
It is for leaving the smell of the desert with her,
to remind her of home one last time.

Suitcase of Saints

There was no saints' table in his house.

There was not even a crucifix on the wall.

No candle was burning.

He said, "I keep the key to the old church.

Every Sunday I go to the old church and pray,

and when they have mass in the new church I go there too.

So, I have no need for saints, candles, or crucifix in my house."

He tells a story.

"One day I was trying to get to Ajo.

I found no ride so I started walking.

Along the way I saw something laying in the bushes in a wash.

I climbed into the wash to take a closer look.

It was a valise. A brown valise. The old style ones.

I lifted it slightly. It was heavy with its load.

My mind quickly tried to imagine what might be in it.

Clothes? Maybe money. Maybe body parts, you know how bad people are
these days.

After some hesitation I opened the latch.

Inside it were saint statues. All kinds.

There was the Virgin of Guadalupe, a Santo Niño, the Holy Family, St. Francis,
St. Martin, St. Peter, the Virgin Mary, and Christ.

There were strands of rosary, all shapes, colors, and colored ribbons, the kind
from Magdalena.

I imagined how they got there.

Surely no one threw them away. It would be wrong.

Perhaps they fell out of someone's truck when they were moving. Surely that
is what must have happened.

They just fell out and the owners didn't realize it until it was too late.

Perhaps they even tried looking for them, but the grass was hiding them.

I'm sure they felt badly about it.

They must have prayed for forgiveness.

No one could have just thrown them out."

He struggles to convince himself.

And then there was another time.

"Oh yes, we were the best Catholics.

We walked from Ajo to Gila Bend to Yuma and places in between.

We walked to Quitobaquito there at Organ Pipe and on down to Rocky Point.

And all the while we carried an extra suitcase just for the saints."

This is what she said with some indignation.

"Yeah, we were very good Catholics, we didn't know any better.

My mother, she didn't know. She had so many saints and bottles of holy water
She carried them, sometimes on horseback, but mostly on foot.
Every evening, wherever we stopped, she opened her suitcase
and set the saints out.
She had St. Francis, the Virgin of Guadalupe, St. Martin, St. Peter, the Holy
   Family.
It's funny, I still remember all their names,
even though I don't believe any more," she said with a smile.
"I don't know whatever happened to that suitcase full of saints.
I had it for a long time.
Maybe one of my daughters took it, a remembrance of their grandma.
I don't know.
No, I don't know whatever happened to it."

Kots

ʾAlwiːlto ʾamt ʾam o ciah
Heg ʾo ʾaṣ cem hekid ʾeḍgid g huk.
Heg ʾat s-keːg o naːto g kots.
Heg ʾo ʾeḍgid g hikckakuḍ.
Heg ʾo ʾeḍgid g klalwos.
Heg ʾo ʾeḍgid g tohă maːsidakuḍ.
Cewĭ miːsa ʾo ʾam keːṣc.
Geʾe ʾo tloːgi.

Ñia, heg ʾamt ʾam o ciah.
Heg ʾat s-keːg o naːto g kots.
Hegai kots mat ʾab o keːkk ha-moʾoṣ ʾab.
Hegai kots mat ʾan ʾab o ʾe-bei k o kekiwua g ʾoks.
Hegai kots mat g m-nanwoj ʾan o taːt

44

hab ṣa masma mat ʼan ha-gegkio ʼan o ha-taːt.

Hegai kots mat ʼab ʼab o ha-naːnaggia g losalo,

mat ʼan ʼab o ha-wuː g lilstoñ mat ʼab ha-ui Maliːna ʼab.

Hegai kots mo ḍ s-keːg cekṣañ.

Hegai kots mamt g ʼAlwiːlto ʼam o ciah.

Nopi hegai cem hekid ʼeḍgid g huk.

Nopi hegai cem hekid s-keːg nantoḍ g kots

Hot Tortillas

During the summer she makes tortillas in a very hot kitchen.
The air temperature is 115 outside,
inside her kitchen this heat is magnified by a wood-burning stove.
Her sweat quickly beads on her forehead and begins a journey down her face.
She leans her head inward and rubs her chin against her shoulder,
temporarily shoring the trickle.
If one of us is around she asks us to wipe the sweat when it doesn't journey
   down her face but runs into her eyes.
All the while she continues the rhythm of her tortilla-making.
With whispered movements she throws the spherical, airlike dough back and
   forth.
Dough, paper thin and perfectly shaped.
They say a measure of a good tortilla maker is if you can read a newspaper
   through it.

We wipe sweat while she keeps working.

When she finishes she goes in the other room to cool off.

She sits there in silence.

Letting her body temperature fall to a normal rate.

The mix of a cooler air temperature and her body heat

allows her to sweat even more.

A cape of wetness emerges around her shoulders and neck.

Her mind and body release themselves from the focus of the heat.

Most of us know better than to disturb her.

Waila Music

It is 1:30 A.M.
Sleep won't come.
She listens to music.
O'odham waila music, San Antonio Rose,
a wild saxophone and accordion.
In her mind she dances.
She dances with a handsome cowboy.
His hat is white, his boots are dusty.
They turn in rhythm together.
They don't miss a beat.
Their hearts beat in sync.
Their sweat is mixed as one.

The earthen dance floor beneath them,
the stars and the moon above them.
That rhythm, that rhythm,
it makes them one.

Deer Dance Exhibition

Question: Can you tell us about what he is wearing?

Well, the hooves represent the deer's hooves,

the red scarf represents the flowers from which he ate,

the shawl is for the skin.

The cocoons make the sound of the deer walking on leaves and grass.

Listen.

Question: What is that he is beating on?

It's a gourd drum. The drum represents the heartbeat of the deer.

Listen.

When the drum beats, it brings the deer to life.

We believe the water the drum sits in is holy. It is life.

Go ahead, touch it.

Bless yourself with it.

It is holy. You are safe now.

Question: How does the boy become a dancer?

He just knows. His mother said he had dreams when he was just a little boy.

You know how that happens. He just had it in him.

Then he started working with older men who taught him how to dance.

He has made many sacrifices for his dancing even for just a young boy.

The people concur, "Yes, you can see it in his face."

Question: What do they do with the money we throw them?

Oh, they just split it among the singers and dancer.

They will probably take the boy to McDonald's for a burger and fries.

The men will probably have a cold one.

It's hot today, you know.

Uncle Stories

His uncle tells stories,
stories he carelessly cups in his memory.
His stories are of adventures and conquests.
His memories slosh into one another, mixing
and discoloring each other.
At times canceling each other out.
But nonetheless, they were good stories.

His aunt's stories on the other hand are of loneliness, waiting,
anxiety, and the pain of loving alone.
Her memories are finely etched with painful strokes.
The sharp points of each one leave their marks.
She feels her memories, and sometimes softly cries for no reason at all.

One-Sided Conversation

He is hard of hearing,
and so am I.
He only hears part of what I say,
and I miss half of what he says.
So we overcompensate and talk twice as much,
with the hope that we may capture the whole.

Musical Retrospective

That summer she intended to listen to her entire collection of Bob Dylan.
The fortieth anniversary collection of his work. It was a time of retrospection.
The retrospection included "bootlegged" recordings found in a small music
   shop.
Some sixteen-plus hours of music on digital recording.

She believes she can hear spit on the harmonica.
She thinks she can feel the vibration of guitar strings.
She knows she can feel the pain in his voice.
She believes the stories his songs tell.
. . . turn, turn, turn, turn.
She lets this man's voice carry her away, away to a place for the drifting,
and the damaged.

He tells stories of loves lost and loves found, of the mixed and confused and
the colors they saw.
She begins at the beginning everytime she listens to her collection,
and so it's the reason she has yet to listen to all of the songs.
Her daughter is exasperated with her, and says, "You're going to die before you
listen to all of them if you start at the beginning each time."
She wants no distractions from his song, stories, his rhythm, and his blues.

In the kitchen there was a small white radio above the table.
Her mother listened to Mexican music from Phoenix in the mornings.
And when her mother was finished in the kitchen, she and her brothers and
sisters listened to rock and roll and country western.
In the room she shared with her sisters, music came over an old round-
shouldered green radio they bought at a used appliance store.
When they were older a special gift from their father, a transistor radio.
Her brother tied the little radio to his waist as they walked the rows of cotton,
chopping weeds during the summer.
They walked alongside each other, row by row, held together with songs.
The drudgery of such work softened with music.
Older workers had larger transistor radios with elaborate systems of carrying
them so they were out of the way of their work.

She seemed to always have music.
She remembers her brother saving money for a 45 rpm record player on layaway
and ordering 45 rpm records by mail.
The records arrived before the player was paid for.
A pastime was her brother reading the labels of his 45 rpm records,
what was on the hit side and what was on side "B."

55

At one point she could have won any TV contest naming the hits from
    the '60s,
and knowing what was on side "B."
At night she fell asleep to music.
She didn't dream about the songs, they merely carried her to deep,
soothing unconsciousness.
She didn't know they would be what would begin to tell her what she
    remembers.

People on Wayward Journeys
(Russian Thistle, Russian Tumbleweed)

They have no use for traffic lights
or crosswalks.
They take fate into their own hands
and roll across streets
in Chandler, Mesa, Coolidge,
and other cotton-field-infested towns.

Many become traffic statistics
under the wheels of Ford pickup trucks.
Luckier ones become temporary hood ornaments
and additions to car grills.

They make trails across the desert,
to the reservation,
they know no boundaries.
They journey from village to village

as if going for visits over coffee.
On Saturday afternoons
they roll early into the village dance,
semi-invited guests.

At night,
the meeting place is along horse corrals.
There most meet their destiny.

A few lucky ones will have winds
to set them free.
To continue their wayward journeys.
Origins unknown.
Destinations unclear.

Ba : ban Ganhu Ge Ci:pia

Ba:ban ganhu ge ci:pia
Ba:ban ganhu ge ci:pia
Kut 'am hema meḍk 'am ha-kakk'e
Kut 'am hema meḍk 'am ha-kakk'e
Ba: mt o ci:pia?
Kut 'am hema meḍk 'am ha-kakk'e
Wa ṣa 'an wo:po ṣon 'oidag

Coyotes moving along over there
Coyotes moving along over there
Someone go over there and ask them
Someone go over there and ask them
Where are you guys moving to?
Running along the foothills

Running along the foothills
Someone go over there and ask them
Someone go over there and ask them
Where are you guys moving to?
With baby's new tenny shoes
And her Merle Haggard and Hank Williams tapes
in the Bashas' grocery bag
And his cowboy boots in another
All worldly goods
Packed up
Moving
Kut 'am hema meḍk 'am ha-kakk'e
Kut 'am hema meḍk 'am ha-kakk'e
Ba: mt o ci:pia?
Someone go over there and ask them
Where are you guys moving to?

Dog Dreams

(for Gloria)

The dog lies in the grass behind the house.
The grass partially covering him,
bending and blowing against him in a cold winter wind.
He curls inside himself for warmth.
His muzzle breathes the only warmth around,
breathes into his chest as he insulates from the cold.
His mind drifts back to more primal times.
He dreams of his ancestors who might have lain on the cold tundra
with only the follicles of their fur to keep them warm.
They lay waiting for the sunlight,
sunlight still an entire season in coming.

And then there was my sister who had two dogs.
She didn't give them names, they just assumed they had names.

She lives along dirt roads where the dogs have tendencies
to chase anything moving.
The two dogs in particular chased cars.
And when they did this she yelled at the first dog, "Come here!"
and at the second dog, "You too!"
And like other historical linguistic accidents of naming,
the dogs assumed their names were "Come here" and "You too."
And so it was.
The only time the names cause confusion is with reprimands such as,
"Get out of here! Come here!"

S-ke:g S-he:pi

The Pleasant Cold

Morning Air

The early morning air,
enveloped in heavy moisture.
I go outside and it lays on my shoulders.
I go about my business,
carrying the morning air
for the rest of the day.

The South Corner

My body is in line.
It is at its darkest point,
but only for a short time.
Not enough time for madness or temporary depression to set in.
The darkest point is only a brief window of opportunity.
Opportunity for sadness, loneliness, falling out of love and other states
   associated with the lack of light.
But before the opportunity can be taken, the shadows turn.
The light becomes stronger,
pulling me toward it.
The warmth, the promise it holds.
And so I begin another cycle,
along with the animals, the plants, the oceans and winds
and all that feel this same pull.

I come into balance.

I begin again.

It is only December twenty-second and it is already starting to feel like summer.

Kitchen Sink

The light from the kitchen-door window comes through in a special way.
I can see the seasons change in my kitchen sink.
The movement of the sun is shadowed in that sink.
During the afternoon the sink is full with sunlight.
Not necessarily a good time to be washing dishes.
Later in the summer there is a sense of urgency as the shadow gets longer and
     begins to slant
as the sunlight starts to edge out of the sink.
I pretend the sunlight is going down the drain.
The light cannot be stopped by the plug in the drain.
It seeps down around the inner seal where water cannot go,
becoming a part of the darkness that is always a part of drains and pipes.
Winter is coming.
The air is probably cooler already.
I know this because of my sink.

68

Lard for Moisturizer

I turn the vertical blinds,

attempting to capture the southern light.

The sun is now at the south corner.

The December wind is cold,

magnifying the weakness of the sun's light.

This light is difficult to contrast

to the searing, still heat of three months ago.

I think of that heat now, but I can't really remember it.

I welcome the gentle warmth of the winter sun.

With this sunlight I think of home and the activity that moves to the east side
   of the house,

to catch the weak winter morning sun.

My father sits on that side for hours doing small repairs.

My mother and her laundry tubs move to that side also.

Bent over her washtubs of clothes, her back to the sun.

Arms moving back and forth washing, pulling on the rays of the sun.

My sisters and I hang out clothes,

being grateful only that it isn't raining.

Sun and winter wind dry the clothes quickly.

The only casualty of this work is our hands.

Hot water, cold water rinse, cold wind, and mild dry sun.

As outdoor people our parents

found small relief in lotions and moisturizers for the skin.

Our family kept the Jergens lotion people in business, we used to say.

Early in December moisturizing lotions were fine, but by January and February
   we were ready for the hard stuff, petroleum jelly.

Our parents went to bed each night with a slight sheen of grease on their
   hands and face.

We did the same.

A minor epidermal comfort.

My sisters and I laugh about one aunt who doesn't even bother with moisturiz-
   ing lotion

or even petroleum jelly, she goes straight for *lard*.

We've all seen her do this.

When she makes her tortilla dough

with the last step she greases each ball of dough.

As she finishes, any lard left over she simply rubs into her hands as she would
   lotion.

My sister mimics and exaggerates the description,

showing us how she rubs the lard on her face, arms,

and then lifts her skirt and rubs a healthy handful on her brown, chapped
   knees.

Ocean Power

Moon Games

The moon is full.

The moon and the ocean play their games.

They rush at one another.

At night my daughter and I sleep well,

oblivious to the games going on outside our tent.

Our bodies in comfortable rhythm with the movements of oceans and moons.

Movements of unimaginable quantities of water,

water just outside our tent flap

and waters thousands of miles away.

Ocean waters newly formed, waters thousands of years old.

And lunar pulls that have traveled around a universe unfathomable.

We are lulled to a deeper sleep rocked like babies.

My husband on the other hand is restless.

He turns in his sleep at every thundering crash of wave.

The noise is deafening to him.

The activity wakes him.

In the morning he asks, "Did you hear the ocean last night?"

He says, "I got up and looked at it to see what was wrong."

Like a Picture Postcard

The azure blue water was like a postcard.
She said, "It looks like a picture of Tahiti or the Virgin Islands
with that boat sitting out there like that."

The water was clear that weekend.
The people on the boat had been traveling for four years on that 4th of July.
Four years on a sixty-foot boat with white sails.
They left from Detroit down the St. Lawrence Seaway and haven't been back
    since.

Of course we asked, "How much longer are you going to be sailing around?"
"Until we can't stand to be on the boat any longer or until we kill each other,
    whichever comes first." They had pat answers for all the typical questions
    asked of people living on boats.
"What do you do all day on the boat?"

75

She is remodeling rooms, refinishing the wood.
He repairs things daily just to keep the boat moving.
They were like a picture on a postcard.

But down below she rocks to the rhythm of the sea
as she softly cries.
She misses simple things,
a walk down a sidewalk lined with trees.
Sitting on a couch next to a warm fire.
The smell of burning pine.
The cool stirring of a winter breeze.
The bright colors of a clean grocery store.
Her skin is continually tanned, dry, always with a layer of salt.
Her hair she knows is too dry, it will never be the same again.
She is convinced her feet have gotten wider from not wearing shoes.
Her hands are rough and big from manual labor.

She misses their friends, whose letters and messages catch up with them when
    they are lucky.
She misses talking to her sisters and her mother.
She has never been really close to her mother,
but thinks when she gets back she'll change that.
For conversation she only has her husband.
They talk about the regular progress of their individual projects.
Her refinishing and sanding and his repairs on sails and rigging.
He reports on the status of
their private sewer company
their private water company

their private fuel company

This is what he likes to call them.

At night she looks into the blackest sky,

and when she doesn't cry she convinces herself their journey is the great
  getaway.

no more traffic

no more bills to pay

no more mother to fight with

no more overcrowding,

at least this is what she convinces herself.

She says this out loud to herself with the ocean and the stars as her witnesses.

For him, well, it is one of those "man" things.

Something he wanted to do, was able to, and so did it.

He didn't want to admit that he was happy to come ashore.

He didn't want to admit the pleasure of having company other than his wife's.

He was happy for her, for her distraction.

They came on shore every evening to have dinner with the campers.

He seemed eager for the company of other men, she, for other women.

On July 4th we all shared the brief fireworks provided by the Australian family
  now living in Hermosillo.

The couple from the boat had their own anniversary to celebrate.

Four years on the ocean.

It seemed they were sad that we would all be leaving the beach soon to head
  further inland.

And they further out to sea on their way south.

As we left we gave them fresh vegetables that would be confiscated at the
  border
and our leftover fuel for their inflatable.
He was the only one who came on shore that morning.
We wished him and his wife well for a continued safe journey.

She was on the boat alone.
The smell of turpentine, wood oil, and damp sea air to her distract.
She did not care that they looked like a picture on a postcard.

Under the Sea

(for Christina)

"Take it from me
under the sea
under the sea
it's so much better
down where it's wetter"

If you take three seashells
because they are pretty,
throw back two.
If you go into the water
make sure that you smile.
If you turn your back to the ocean,
say "excuse me."
If you happen to have desert flowers in hand,

put them on the ocean waves and let them ride to sea.
If you leave the ocean water,
make sure you are grateful for being safe.
If you are so inclined,
you may create a poem.
If you are so inclined you may
dream a song.
If you are so inclined and you feel ready,
you may ask for something from the ocean.
If you are so inclined you may not discuss this with anyone
except the power of the ocean.
If you are so inclined to ask me when you will be ready,
don't ask,
you will know.
For you and I agree,
"Under the sea
under the sea
it's so much better
down where it's wetter."

Ka:cim Ṣu:dagĭ

S-wegima 'am ka:c g ha'icu hiosig
S-ce:daghim 'am ka:c g ha'icu hiosig
S-i:bhaghim 'am ka:c g ha'icu hiosig
'Am ka:c heg da:m ge'e ka:cim ṣu:dagĭ
Heg wui 'att 'i-ul g s-ke:g ha'icu cegĭtodag
Heg wui 'att 'i-ul g s-ap ta:hadag
Heg wui 'att 'i-ul g 'i:mdag
'Am 'att ta:t g ge'e ka:cim ṣu:dagĭ
k 'amjeḍ 'am 'aṣ 'i-dagĭto.

Red-colored blossoms
Green-colored blossoms
Purple-colored blossoms
All float above the laying water

Toward it we extend only good thoughts
Toward it we extend only good feelings
Toward it we extend kinship
We touched this laying water
and then we left it alone.

Ocean Power

Words cannot speak your power.
Words cannot speak your beauty.
Grown men with dry fear in their throats
watch the water come closer and closer.
Their driver tells them, "It's just the ocean,
it won't get you, watch it, it will roll away again.

Men who had never seen the ocean
it was hard not to have the fear that sits in the pit of the stomach.
Why did they bring us this way?
Other times we crossed on the desert floor.
That land of hot dry air
where the sky ends at the mountains.
That land that we know.

That land where the ocean has not touched for thousands of years.
We do not belong here,
this place with the sky too endless.
This place with the water too endless.
This place with air too thick and heavy to breathe.
This place with the roll and roar of thunder always playing to your ears.

We are not ready to be here.
We are not prepared in the old way.
We have no medicine.
We have not sat and had our minds walk through the image
of coming to this ocean.
We are not ready.
We have not put our minds to what it is we want to give to the ocean.
We do not have cornmeal, feathers, nor do we have songs and prayers ready.
We have not thought what gift we will ask from the ocean.
Should we ask to be song chasers
Should we ask to be rainmakers
Should we ask to be good runners
or should we ask to be heartbreakers.
No, we are not ready to be here at this ocean.

Afterword

On the Tohono O'odham

This afterword is for readers not familiar with the Southwest tribe of people who call themselves Tohono O'odham, or Desert People. It also provides references for interested readers who want further information on the Tohono O'odham, formerly known as the Papago.

The O'odham population numbers somewhere between 18,000 and 21,000. The people live in southern Arizona and northern Sonora, Mexico, residing primarily on three reservations: Wa:k, or San Xavier, near Tucson; the main reservation where the tribal agency is in the town of Sells, Arizona; and a third reservation near Gila Bend, Arizona. Many O'odham also live in or near the various border towns of Casa Grande, Ajo, Florence, and Eloy, and in rural communities such as Stanfield, Arizona. Others live in the major cities of Tucson and Phoenix.

By virtue of population and land, the Tohono O'odham tribe is significant in the United States. Its population and reservation size is second in the Southwest only to the Navajo nation. Because the Tohono O'odham is a desert tribe, however, it is not commonly known among non-Indians. Contemporary socio-logical and ethnographic information on the O'odham is available in a book by Bernard Fontana and John P. Schaefer, *Of Earth and Little Rain* (University of Arizona Press, 1990). A historical account is provided in *Sharing the Desert: The Tohono O'odham in History* by Winston Erickson (University of Arizona Press, 1994).

The current Tohono O'odham reservations are in the general area that was the indigenous territory of the people. As a result, the O'odham negotiate politi-cally and socially around the international border between the United States and Mexico that divides Tohono O'odham land and people. The poem "Ocean Power" is about two O'odham men who came too close to the ocean as they were being deported back to Mexico from Arizona.

Among the Tohono O'odham is a distinct "band" of O'odham who call them-selves Hia-ceḍ O'odham, or Sand Papago. This group had its indigenous lands in the westernmost part of Arizona, including what is now the world-famous Organ Pipe National Monument. Other parts of their territory extend into northern Sonora, Mexico, including Rocky Point on the ocean. The poem "Suitcase Full of Saints" is about members of the band of Hia-ceḍ O'odham residing in Ajo and Gila Bend. There is little published material on the Hia-ceḍ O'odham. However, readers can learn more about them in an oral history proj-ect on the Sand Papago that I collected in 1985. This project was funded by the Division of Archeology, Western Archeological and Conservation Center, National Park Service, Tucson, Arizona, and is available from that office. The only other collection on the Sand Papago is "The Quitobaquito Cemetery and Its History" by Fillman Bell, Keith Anderson, and Yvonne G. Stewart (1980), also available at the Western Archeological Center.

The Tohono O'odham language is part of the Uto-Aztecan language family. Related languages in the Southwest include Pima, Yaqui, and Hopi; other languages are found in Mexico and farther south. The O'odham's closest linguistic cousins, the Pima tribe of Arizona, live near Phoenix. The O'odham language is still spoken by many members of the tribe. The language is rich in many forms of oral texts. The speakers represent various regional dialects—all mutually intelligible.

Written O'odham is a relatively new creation. There are two significant writing systems for the language; both orthographies are used for scholarly and creative publications. My book, *A Papago Grammar*, and the *Papago/Pima–English, English–Papago/Pima Dictionary* by Dean Saxton, Lucille Saxton, and Susie Enos (both published by the University of Arizona Press in 1983), offer specific information on written O'odham.

The O'odham live in the Sonoran Desert, which has its own seasons. It has long periods of dry, hot weather with temperatures exceeding 110 degrees. This extreme heat is then relieved with gentle rains in the winter—gentle rains that sometimes become wild and dangerous. The poem "The Floods of 1993 and Others" is the story of a harsh winter rain that flooded the desert. Otherwise, when the rains are gentle, the saguaro cactus quietly pulls in the moisture and stands plump, holding the moisture, ready for the next inevitable dry period.

The best rains, though, are the summer rains, rains also known as the "monsoons." These rains come in mid-July and last into August. This is the time of renewal for the O'odham. The summer is an important time, and according to some, the beginning of the O'odham year. The poems "Wind" and "O'odham Dances" include references to certain O'odham rituals that take place in the summer. In the introduction, the mention of relatives who "knew how to live toward the ocean" and who participated in "pulling down the clouds" refers to various rituals of what some call "making rain," and the O'odham call "fixing the earth."

Further reading on some of these topics can be found in any of the works of Ruth Murray Underhill, an early ethnographer of the Papago. Her 1938 book on O'odham ritual songs and speeches, *Singing for Power: The Song Magic of the Papago Indians of Southern Arizona*, was reprinted in 1993 by the University of Arizona Press as a Sun Tracks book; it includes a foreword that I wrote. Other extensive publications on O'odham ritual and ceremony include the work of Donald Bahr, an anthropologist and linguist specializing in O'odham and Pima songs and speeches. Bahr's collection, *Papago-Pima Ritual Oratory: A Study of Three Texts* (San Francisco Indian Historian Press, 1975), is one of the most comprehensive works on American Indian ritual. It was collected among the O'odham in the native language. His other work on O'odham ritual was the editing of Ruth Underhill's transcriptions of her early collections, some of which appeared in *Singing for Power*. Bahr, Underhill, and O'odham medicine men and specialists "reconstructed" many of the songs and speeches from her O'odham transcriptions and represented the speeches in O'odham. This work is available in the collection *Rainhouse and Ocean: Speeches for the Papago Year* (Museum of Northern Arizona, 1979), edited by Underhill, Bahr, Baptisto Lopez, Jose Pancho, and David Lopez. O'odham traditional texts and translations also appear in Dean and Lucille Saxton's collection, *Legends and Lore of the Papago and Pima Indians* (University of Arizona Press, 1973, 1984). Other O'odham traditional texts and songs with translations have been published in the anthology on Arizona tribal traditional and contemporary writing, *The South Corner of Time: Hopi, Navajo, Papago, Yaqui Tribal Literature*, edited by Larry Evers (University of Arizona Press, 1981, 1993). Unfortunately, the works of Bahr, Bahr and Underhill et al., Saxton and Saxton, and Evers are currently out of print. These works can be found in major libraries, however.

▪ ▪

Finally, having read much of what various researchers and writers have to say about the Tohono O'odham, I find one observation that they make about the people to be true and particularly poignant: The O'odham lack grand ritual paraphernalia that call for attention. Instead they wear muted white clay paint on their faces and bodies. The songs of the people are accompanied by hard wood rasps that succeed only in making music that is swallowed by the desert floor. The drumming is on overturned woven baskets, sounds that also reverberate only short distances. The people have no grand, colorful powwows and such social dancing. Instead, their dancing is quiet barefoot skipping and shuffling on dry dirt—movements that cause dust to rise quietly toward the atmosphere, dust that the people believe helps to form rain clouds.

About the Author

Ofelia Zepeda is a member of the Tohono O'odham (formerly Papago) tribe of Arizona. She was born and raised in Stanfield, Arizona, a rural cotton-farming community near the Tohono O'odham reservation. She holds a master's degree and a doctorate in linguistics from the University of Arizona.

Dr. Zepeda authored the first grammar of the Tohono O'odham language, *A Papago Grammar* (University of Arizona Press, 1983). She also has been a contributor to several collections of Native American literature, including *The South Corner of Time* (1981), *Returning the Gift* (1994), and *Home Places* (1995), all in the Sun Tracks series published by the University of Arizona Press.

Ofelia Zepeda is Professor of Linguistics at the University of Arizona, Tucson. She has taught courses on the O'odham language, American Indian linguistics, American Indian language education, and creative writing for native speakers of Southwest Indian languages. She is currently series editor of Sun Tracks.